# Knowledge Overload

## Navigating Unwanted Information

By

Dr. Robert J. Coleman

Copyright © Dr. Robert J. Coleman 2023. All rights reserved.

Before this document is duplicated or reproduced in any manner, the publisher's consent must be gained. Therefore, the contents within can neither be stored electronically, transferred, nor kept in a database. Neither in Part nor full can the document be copied, scanned, faxed, or retained without approval from the publisher or creator.

# Table of contents

Introduction

Chapter 1: The Rise of Knowledge Overload

Chapter 2: The Psychology of Information Processing

Chapter 3: Cultivating Information Literacy

Chapter 4: Managing Information Overload

Chapter 5: Digital Detox and Mindfulness

Chapter 6: Nurturing Intellectual Curiosity

Chapter 7: Building Healthy Information Consumption Habits

Chapter 8: The Future of Knowledge and Information

Conclusion

# Introduction

In today's interconnected world, rapid advancements in technology have ushered in an era of unparalleled access to information. The digital revolution has transformed the way we acquire knowledge, placing a vast array of information at our fingertips. From news articles and research papers to social media updates and online forums, the possibilities for learning seem endless. However, amidst this abundance of knowledge, a new challenge has emerged: knowledge overload.In "Knowledge Overload: Finding Clarity in a Sea of Information," we embark on a journey to explore the implications of this phenomenon and discover strategies for effectively navigating through the overwhelming flood of information. In this book, we delve deep into the psychological and cognitive aspects of information processing, unravel the consequences of knowledge overload on both our personal and professional lives, and unveil practical techniques for managing and leveraging the wealth of information available to us. The sheer volume of data bombarding us from various sources can be daunting and lead to a sense of confusion and mental fatigue. The deluge of information also presents challenges in discerning what is accurate, relevant, and trustworthy. As a result, the pursuit of knowledge can become a double-edged sword, simultaneously empowering and paralyzing us. Our intention is not to cast a negative light on knowledge itself or discourage intellectual growth. Instead, we aim to empower readers to become discerning consumers of information, capable of sifting through the noise to identify quality content, make informed decisions, and maintain a healthy balance in their pursuit of knowledge. In this book, we will explore the importance of information literacy, critical thinking, and effective information management in an era where the boundaries between fact and fiction are increasingly blurred. Moreover, we will discuss the profound impact of knowledge overload on our overall well-being and offer practical strategies for preserving our mental and emotional health amidst the relentless onslaught of information. In the age of knowledge overload, it is crucial to find ways to maintain equilibrium. We will delve into topics such as digital detoxes, mindfulness practices, nurturing intellectual curiosity, and developing healthy information consumption habits. By providing these tools, we aim to assist readers in finding a sense of balance and fulfillment in an era of knowledge abundance.

As we embark on this exploration, we invite you, the reader, to reflect on your relationship with knowledge and consider how knowledge overload has affected you personally. Together, let us navigate the vast sea of information, transform it into a source of empowerment rather than overwhelm it, and reclaim our ability to thrive in the age of knowledge abundance. By embracing the strategies and insights shared in this book, we can not only alleviate the burdens of knowledge overload but also unlock the true potential that lies within our interconnected world

# Chapter 1:

# The Rise of Knowledge Overload

In this chapter, we will delve into the origins and drivers of knowledge overload in the digital age, focusing on the exponential growth of information accessibility and production. The advent of the internet and digital technology has revolutionized the way we access and disseminate information, resulting in an overwhelming abundance of knowledge available to billions of people worldwide. We will explore the implications of this information explosion on various aspects of our daily lives and discuss the challenges it poses.

The internet and digital platforms have transformed the landscape of information. Online platforms, social media, and digital content have facilitated the creation and distribution of vast amounts of information. The ease of publishing and sharing content has contributed to the rapid expansion of available knowledge. We will examine how this growth has impacted our ability to filter and process information effectively, as well as the potential consequences of being constantly bombarded with an immense volume of data.

## 1. The Social Media Effect:

Social media platforms play a significant role in the dissemination and consumption of information in today's digital age. In this chapter, we will delve into the impact of social media on knowledge overload. We will explore the algorithms and attention economy that underlie these platforms, driving the constant flow of information. Additionally, we will discuss how social media contributes to the formation of filter bubbles and echo chambers, limiting exposure to diverse perspectives and reinforcing existing beliefs.
The viral nature of the content on social media platforms can lead to the rapid spread of information, often without thorough fact-checking or verification. This phenomenon can give rise to

misinformation and disinformation, further complicating the quest for reliable knowledge. We will explore the challenges associated with viral content and discuss strategies for critically evaluating information in an era where falsehoods can easily gain traction.

## 2. The Tyranny of Choice:

In the digital age, we face an overwhelming array of choices when it comes to consuming information. This abundance of options can lead to decision fatigue and cognitive overload. In this chapter, we will explore the psychological and cognitive aspects of decision-making in the face of information overload.We will delve into concepts such as choice paralysis, where an excess of options hinders decision-making processes, and the paradox of choice, which suggests that having more choices does not necessarily lead to increased satisfaction. Understanding these phenomena will help us navigate the complexities of decision-making and develop strategies to prioritize information effectively, ensuring that we can make informed choices without becoming overwhelmed.

## 3. The Fragmentation of Knowledge:

The digital age has brought about the fragmentation of knowledge into specialized domains. While this specialization has enabled in-depth understanding in specific areas, it has also made it challenging to gain a holistic view of complex topics. In this chapter, we will explore the consequences of knowledge fragmentation and its impact on our ability to comprehend and synthesize information.

We will discuss the importance of interdisciplinary learning as a means to overcome the limitations of fragmented knowledge. By integrating insights from different fields, we can develop a broader understanding of complex issues and foster creativity and innovation. Understanding the benefits and challenges associated with knowledge specialization will help us navigate the vast landscape of information more effectively.

## 4. The Challenge of Information Quality:

The abundance of information in the digital age does not guarantee its quality or accuracy. In this chapter, we will examine the challenges posed by misinformation, fake news, and the spread of disinformation campaigns. We will explore the factors that contribute to these challenges, such as confirmation bias and the erosion of trust in traditional information sources.

Developing the ability to critically evaluate information is crucial in an era where misinformation can easily proliferate. We will discuss strategies for fact-checking, verifying sources, and cultivating a healthy skepticism to ensure that we can discern reliable information from falsehoods. By equipping ourselves with these tools, we can navigate the complex landscape of information with greater confidence and make informed decisions.

we have examined the rise of knowledge overload in the digital age. We explored the information explosion, the impact of social media, the challenges of decision-making, the fragmentation of knowledge, and the issues surrounding information quality. By understanding the factors that have contributed to knowledge overload, we can begin to develop strategies and approaches to navigate through this overwhelming sea of information.

In the following chapters, we will delve deeper into the psychological aspects of information processing, explore practical techniques for managing information overload, and discuss ways to cultivate a healthy relationship with knowledge in an era of abundance. By applying these insights, we can harness the power of information without succumbing to its overwhelming nature, ensuring that we make the most of the digital age's vast knowledge resources.

# Chapter 2:

# The Psychology of Information Processing

In this extensive chapter, we will embark on a journey into the intricate realm of psychological aspects surrounding information processing. We aim to unravel the mysteries of how these processes influence our interactions with knowledge, leading to a deeper understanding of how we navigate the overwhelming influx of information that bombards us daily. By delving into the depths of our cognitive processes, we can uncover invaluable insights that will enable us to develop strategies for optimizing our information processing and, in turn, make more informed decisions.

At the core of our exploration lies the concept of attention, a fundamental cognitive function that shapes our perception of the world and determines which pieces of information we notice and engage with. We will venture into the realms of selective attention, delving into its complexities and examining the factors that influence our attentional filters. By gaining a profound understanding of how our brains prioritize and filter information, we will cultivate a heightened awareness of our attentional biases. Armed with this awareness, we can then develop techniques to hone our focus, directing it toward relevant and meaningful content that aligns with our goals and intentions.

## 3. Memory and Information Retention:

Memory, an indispensable facet of our cognitive architecture, plays a pivotal role in the acquisition and retention of knowledge. In this comprehensive chapter, we will delve into the multifaceted nature of memory, exploring its various forms such as working memory and long-term memory. Moreover, we will examine how the relentless onslaught of information overload can profoundly impact our ability to encode, store, and retrieve information effectively.

As we navigate the challenges posed by the overwhelming amount of information at our fingertips, strategies for enhancing memory and optimizing information retention become paramount. We will embark on an exploration of these strategies, uncovering techniques that can aid us in mitigating the adverse effects of knowledge overload. By embracing these techniques, we can empower ourselves to encode information more efficiently, store it in a manner that facilitates retrieval, and ultimately bolster our capacity to retain and apply knowledge in meaningful ways.

## 4. Cognitive Biases and Information Processing:

Within the recesses of our minds lie inherent mental shortcuts and tendencies known as cognitive biases. In this expansive chapter, we will embark on an illuminating journey to understand the influence of these biases on our decision-making and information-processing capabilities. We will scrutinize common biases such as confirmation bias, availability heuristic, and anchoring effect, unraveling their mechanisms and shedding light on their pervasive impact.

By unraveling the intricacies of cognitive biases, we arm ourselves with the tools necessary to challenge their grip on our thinking processes. Armed with this knowledge, we can cultivate a heightened awareness of how these biases influence our perception of information, allowing us to engage in critical thinking and counteract their potential pitfalls. Through this process, we open ourselves up to more nuanced and balanced perspectives, enabling us to make more informed decisions in an increasingly complex world.

## 5. Filtering and Sensemaking:

Amidst the vast sea of information that engulfs us, the need for effective strategies for filtering and sensemaking becomes undeniable. In this expansive chapter, we embark on a voyage to explore a myriad of techniques and frameworks that can assist us in navigating this overwhelming landscape. We will venture into the realm of information triage, a method that empowers us to swiftly assess the relevance and reliability of the information we encounter.

Furthermore, we will delve into frameworks such as the CRAAP (Currency, Relevance, Authority, Accuracy, Purpose) test, which provides a systematic approach to evaluating sources. Armed with these tools, we can build an arsenal of strategies to aid us in distinguishing valuable insights from misinformation, empowering us to make more informed judgments and avoid being swayed by the vast array of unreliable information that permeates our digital lives.

## 6. Cognitive Overload and Decision Fatigue:

As we traverse the treacherous terrain of information overload, we encounter the perils of cognitive overload—a state in which our brains become overwhelmed by excessive stimulation. In this crucial chapter, we shine a light on the consequences of cognitive overload, ranging from reduced decision-making abilities to increased mental fatigue. We delve into the mechanisms that underlie these phenomena, fostering a deep understanding of the impact of cognitive overload on our cognitive resources.

To overcome these challenges, we explore strategies for managing cognitive load effectively. Techniques such as chunking information, prioritizing tasks, and taking regular breaks become invaluable tools in optimizing our cognitive resources and alleviating the burdens imposed by information overload. By implementing these strategies, we can navigate the intricate web of knowledge with greater ease, preserving our mental acuity and enhancing our ability to make sound decisions in the face of overwhelming information.

In this extensive exploration of the psychology of information processing, we have traversed the vast landscapes of attention, memory, cognitive biases, filtering, and decision-making. Armed with a newfound understanding of these cognitive processes, we gain valuable insights into our information consumption habits and the challenges we encounter in an era characterized by an overwhelming abundance of knowledge.

By harnessing this knowledge, we equip ourselves with the tools necessary to develop strategies that enhance attention, optimize memory retention, counteract cognitive biases, and effectively filter information. These strategies pave the way for us to navigate the complex world of information with clarity and discernment, enabling us to make more informed decisions and harness the power of knowledge effectively.

In the upcoming chapter, we embark on a practical exploration of techniques for managing information overload and finding a harmonious balance in our digital lives. By merging theoretical insights with practical solutions, we delve into the practical realm, equipping ourselves with strategies that empower us to thrive amidst the vast sea of information while nurturing our well-being in an increasingly interconnected world.

# Chapter 3:

# Cultivating Information Literacy

In today's age of knowledge overload, information literacy has become a critical skill for effectively navigating the vast sea of information and discerning reliable, accurate, and relevant knowledge. In this chapter, we will delve into the concept of information literacy, its significance in our information-rich society, and its practical application in personal, academic, and professional contexts.

Information literacy extends beyond mere access to information; it encompasses the abilities needed to locate, evaluate, interpret, and effectively utilize information. We will explore the core components of information literacy, including information seeking, evaluation, analysis, and application. By developing these competencies, individuals can enhance their capacity to make informed decisions, solve problems, and engage with information in meaningful ways.

## 1. Source Evaluation and Credibility:

A fundamental aspect of information literacy is the ability to evaluate the credibility and reliability of sources. In this chapter, we will explore strategies for assessing the authority, expertise, objectivity, and currency of different sources. Whether it is websites, articles, or social media content, understanding the characteristics of reliable sources is essential for making informed judgments about the information we encounter.

We will delve into various criteria for evaluating sources, such as considering the author's credentials, the publisher's reputation, and the presence of citations and references. Additionally, we will discuss the importance of cross-referencing information and seeking diverse perspectives to gain a more comprehensive understanding of a topic.

## 2. Fact-Checking and Verifying Information:

In the digital landscape, misinformation and false information have become pervasive challenges. In this chapter, we will emphasize the significance of fact-checking and verifying information before accepting it as true. We will explore different fact-checking methodologies, reliable fact-checking organizations, and online tools that can assist in verifying the accuracy of information.

By understanding the principles of fact-checking, individuals can develop a critical mindset and avoid the pitfalls of misinformation. We will also discuss the importance of triangulating information from multiple credible sources to ensure its reliability.

## 3. Critical Thinking and Analysis:

Critical thinking skills are essential for information literacy. In this chapter, we will explore techniques for critically analyzing information, and identifying biases, logical fallacies, and rhetorical devices. By developing these skills, individuals can evaluate the validity and reliability of information and make well-informed judgments.

We will emphasize the importance of questioning assumptions, considering alternative viewpoints, and recognizing the influence of personal biases. Moreover, we will discuss the role of critical thinking in promoting intellectual curiosity, creativity, and independent thought.

## 4. Media Literacy:

In the era of social media and digital news, media literacy plays a vital role in information literacy. This chapter will delve into the importance of understanding media bias, recognizing clickbait and sensationalism, and navigating through filter bubbles. Strategies for developing media literacy skills, including media literacy education and diverse news consumption, will be explored.

By enhancing media literacy, individuals can become more discerning consumers of news and media content. We will discuss techniques for analyzing and interpreting media messages, distinguishing between reliable and unreliable sources, and engaging in constructive online discussions.

## 5. Research Skills and Information Synthesis:

Effective research skills are integral to information literacy. In this chapter, we will explore techniques for conducting thorough research, organizing and synthesizing information, and properly citing sources. These skills enable individuals to delve deeper into topics, evaluate multiple perspectives, and present well-rounded arguments.

We will discuss strategies for formulating research questions, employing appropriate search strategies, and critically evaluating the relevance and reliability of sources. Additionally, we will emphasize the importance of ethical information use, including proper citation practices and respect for intellectual property rights.Cultivating information literacy is essential for navigating the vast landscape of knowledge in the digital age. By developing the skills to evaluate sources, fact-check information, think critically, and engage with media responsibly, individuals can become empowered consumers of knowledge. In this chapter, we have explored the various aspects of information literacy and discussed practical strategies for cultivating these skills. In the following chapters, we will delve into techniques for managing information overload, fostering a healthy information diet, and embracing a mindful approach to knowledge consumption.

## Chapter 4:

## Managing Information Overload

In the era of digital advancements, we find ourselves constantly inundated with an unprecedented amount of information. The ability to effectively manage this information overload has become paramount for maintaining productivity, preserving mental well-being, and making informed decisions. In this chapter, we will delve into practical techniques and strategies that can help us regain control over our digital lives by efficiently managing information overload.

One of the key approaches to managing information overload is through filtering and curating the vast amount of available knowledge. By selectively choosing the sources and topics we engage with, we can reduce the noise and focus on the most relevant and valuable information. Personalized filters, such as advanced search settings and customized news alerts, allow us to narrow down our information intake based on specific criteria. This ensures that we receive updates and news only from sources that align with our interests and needs.

Additionally, utilizing RSS feeds can be immensely helpful in consolidating information from various sources into a single platform. RSS readers enable us to subscribe to our preferred websites, blogs, and publications, consolidating their updates into a single feed. This minimizes the need to visit multiple websites individually, saving time and reducing the likelihood of missing out on important information. Content aggregation tools further enhance our ability to manage information overload. These tools gather and organize content from multiple sources, presenting it in a unified and easily accessible manner. By using such tools, we can efficiently scan through headlines, summaries, and excerpts to quickly identify the content that is most relevant to our interests and goals. This way, we can stay informed without being overwhelmed by the sheer volume of information available.

## 2. Prioritization and Time Management in the Face of Information Overload:

To effectively combat information overload, it is crucial to develop strong prioritization and time management skills. Without these abilities, we may find ourselves constantly overwhelmed and struggling to allocate our attention and resources effectively. In this chapter, we will explore methods and techniques that can assist us in prioritizing information and managing our time more efficiently.

The Eisenhower Matrix, also known as the Urgent-Important Matrix, is a valuable tool for prioritization. It categorizes tasks and information into four quadrants based on their urgency and importance. By categorizing information according to these criteria, we can determine which tasks or sources require immediate attention and which can be deferred or delegated. This approach helps us avoid getting caught up in trivial or non-essential information, allowing us to focus on the most critical and meaningful tasks at hand.

Time blocking is another powerful technique for managing information overload. By setting aside specific blocks of time for different activities, we can establish a structured schedule that ensures dedicated time for consuming and processing information. This technique not only helps in managing the amount of time spent on information intake but also prevents information overload from encroaching on other important aspects of our lives. By allocating fixed time slots for information consumption, we can strike a balance between staying informed and engaging in other essential activities.

Task prioritization techniques, such as the ABC method or the Pareto Principle (also known as the 80/20 rule), can aid in efficiently managing information overload. These approaches involve assigning priorities to tasks or sources based on their importance and potential impact. By focusing on the most significant information and tasks, we can make the most of our limited time and attention, avoiding the feeling of being overwhelmed by the sheer volume of information available.

## 3. Digital Organization and Efficient Information Management:

In the digital age, creating a structured and organized digital environment is essential for effectively managing information overload. Without proper organization and information management systems, finding relevant information can become a time-consuming and mentally draining task. In this chapter, we will explore various techniques for organizing digital files, utilizing note-taking and bookmarking tools, and maintaining a clutter-free digital workspace.

An efficient information management system starts with organizing digital files in a logical and easily navigable manner. By creating appropriate folder structures, using descriptive file names, and implementing consistent naming conventions, we can quickly locate the information we need. Moreover, utilizing search functions and metadata tags within file management systems can significantly enhance our ability to retrieve specific files or information promptly. Note-taking and bookmarking tools are valuable assets in managing information overload. Digital note-taking applications allow us to capture and organize key insights, summaries, and references from various sources. By using tags, categories, or notebooks, we can ensure that our notes are well-organized and easily searchable. Similarly, bookmarking tools enable us to save and categorize web pages, articles, and resources for future reference. These tools not only help us avoid information overload in the present but also provide a valuable repository of knowledge for later use.

Maintaining a clutter-free digital workspace is equally important in managing information overload. A cluttered desktop or an overflowing inbox can contribute to a sense of overwhelm and make it difficult to locate essential information. By organizing files into appropriate folders, regularly archiving or deleting unnecessary emails, and minimizing the number of visible distractions, we can create a focused and efficient digital workspace. This, in turn, enhances our ability to process and manage information effectively.

## 4. Setting Boundaries and Embracing Digital Detoxes:

In today's hyper-connected world, setting boundaries with technology is essential for managing information overload. The constant stream of notifications, emails, and social media updates can quickly become overwhelming, leaving us feeling mentally drained and distracted. In this chapter, we will explore strategies for establishing healthy digital habits, practicing digital detoxes, and creating technology-free zones.

One of the first steps in setting boundaries is establishing designated times for checking emails, social media, and other digital platforms. By allocating specific time slots for these activities, we can prevent information overload from encroaching on other aspects of our lives. For example, dedicating the first and last hour of the workday to email management allows us to prioritize other important tasks during the core productive hours.

Digital detoxes are periods of intentional disconnection from technology, aimed at rejuvenating our mental well-being and regaining control over information consumption. During a digital detox, we can abstain from using electronic devices or restrict our access to specific applications or platforms. This break from constant connectivity enables us to recharge, refocus, and reset our relationship with information. Engaging in activities such as reading books, spending time in nature, or engaging in creative pursuits during these detox periods can further promote a balanced and healthy approach to information consumption.

Creating technology-free zones within our living or working spaces is another effective strategy for managing information overload. By designating specific areas, such as bedrooms, dining areas, or meeting rooms, as technology-free zones, we create opportunities for uninterrupted face-to-face interactions, relaxation, and reflection. These spaces provide a respite from the constant influx of information and allow us to cultivate a greater sense of presence and connection with the physical world.

## 5. Mindful Information Consumption for Clarity and Discernment:

In the face of information overload, practicing mindful information consumption can help us approach knowledge with clarity, discernment, and intentionality. By cultivating a sense of presence and awareness, we can navigate the vast sea of information more effectively and make informed decisions. In this chapter, we will explore the concept of mindful information consumption and various mindfulness practices that can enhance our engagement with information.

Mindful information consumption involves being fully present and engaged with the information at hand. It requires us to be aware of our mental and emotional state while consuming information, as well as the potential biases or assumptions that may influence our interpretation. By cultivating mindfulness, we can approach information with a sense of curiosity, openness, and critical thinking.

Mindfulness practices such as deep breathing exercises, meditation, and mindful reading can significantly enhance our ability to consume information mindfully. Deep breathing exercises help us center ourselves and bring our attention to the present moment before engaging with information. Meditation, whether in the form of focused attention or open awareness, cultivates a greater sense of clarity, calmness, and discernment, enabling us to process information more effectively. Mindful reading involves reading slowly and attentively, allowing us to absorb the content more deeply and critically evaluate its relevance and reliability.

## 6. Developing Selective Consumption Habits for Quality Knowledge:

Developing selective consumption habits is essential for managing information overload effectively. By being intentional about the sources we follow, the content we engage with, and the notifications we allow, we can reduce overwhelm, minimize distractions, and focus on quality knowledge. In this chapter, we will delve into the importance of selective consumption and discuss strategies for cultivating healthy information consumption habits. Being selective about the sources we follow and engage with is crucial for maintaining a high standard of information quality. By critically evaluating the credibility, expertise, and reliability of sources, we can ensure that the information we consume is accurate, trustworthy, and relevant. Subscribing to reputable publications, following experts in specific fields, and participating in trusted online communities can help curate a stream of reliable and valuable information.

Moreover, consciously selecting the content we engage with can prevent information overload and enhance our learning experience. It is essential to choose content that aligns with our interests, goals, and values. By focusing on topics that are personally meaningful and relevant, we can make our information consumption more purposeful and enjoyable. Additionally, being mindful of the format and length of content can help us manage our time and attention more effectively. For instance, opting for long-form articles or in-depth analyses can provide more comprehensive insights compared to fleeting social media updates.

Controlling notifications is another aspect of selective consumption that significantly impacts our information intake. By customizing our notification settings and limiting the number of interruptions, we can reduce the constant bombardment of information and regain control over our attention. Disabling notifications from non-essential applications, muting or unsubscribing from excessive email newsletters, and setting specific times for checking messages can help us establish healthier boundaries with technology.

managing information overload in the digital age is crucial for maintaining productivity, mental well-being, and informed decision-making. By filtering and curating information, prioritizing and managing time effectively, organizing digital files, setting boundaries, practicing digital detoxes, cultivating mindfulness, and developing selective consumption habits, we can regain control over our information consumption. These strategies not only help us navigate the overwhelming sea of information but also promote productivity, well-being, and a balanced approach to knowledge. In the following chapters, we will delve into the importance of nurturing intellectual curiosity and building healthy information consumption habits to further optimize our relationship with knowledge.

## Chapter 5:

## Digital Detox and Mindfulness

In today's technology-driven and information-saturated world, finding moments of respite and cultivating mindfulness have become essential for our overall well-being. In this chapter, we will explore the concept of digital detox and mindfulness as powerful tools for managing information overload, reducing digital dependency, and fostering a healthier relationship with technology and knowledge.

Digital detox refers to a deliberate and temporary disconnection from digital devices and online platforms. In an era where we are constantly bombarded with notifications, messages, and an overwhelming amount of information, taking a step back from technology can be beneficial in numerous ways. By engaging in a digital detox, individuals can reduce stress, improve their mental health, and regain focus and productivity.

We will delve into the reasons why digital detox is important, emphasizing the detrimental effects of constant digital stimulation on our well-being. Research has shown that excessive screen time and constant connectivity can lead to heightened levels of stress, anxiety, and a decreased ability to concentrate. Digital detox provides an opportunity to break free from these negative impacts and reclaim a sense of balance and tranquility.

Furthermore, we will explore different approaches to digital detox, recognizing that there is no one-size-fits-all solution. Some individuals may benefit from short breaks, such as taking regular intervals during the day to disconnect from their devices, while others may find value in longer periods of complete disconnection, such as a weekend or even a week-long break. We will provide practical tips and strategies for implementing a successful digital detox, emphasizing the importance of planning, setting goals, and gradually reducing digital dependency.

## 1. Setting Boundaries with Technology:

Establishing clear boundaries with technology is vital for managing information overload and promoting a healthier digital lifestyle. In this chapter, we will explore various strategies for setting boundaries, enabling individuals to regain control over their technology habits, and create space for more meaningful interactions.

One effective strategy is to create device-free zones in our homes or workplaces. By designating specific areas where technology is not allowed, such as bedrooms or dining areas, we can establish a healthier separation between our digital and offline lives. This separation allows us to fully engage in activities without the distractions and interruptions caused by constant technological connectivity.

Additionally, implementing screen-free periods can be highly beneficial. Designating specific times during the day or week when screens are not used, such as during meals, before bed, or on weekends, helps create a healthier balance and reduces the reliance on digital devices. During these screen-free periods, individuals can engage in activities that promote well-being, such as reading, exercising, spending time in nature, or engaging in hobbies.

Furthermore, establishing technology usage guidelines can help set boundaries. This can involve defining specific times for checking emails or social media, limiting the number of hours spent on screens each day, and consciously allocating time for focused work or leisure activities without any digital distractions. By setting clear guidelines, individuals can regain control over their technology use and avoid falling into the trap of mindless scrolling or constant multitasking.

## 2. Mindfulness in the Digital Age:

Mindfulness, the practice of being fully present and aware of the present moment, is a powerful tool for navigating the digital age and managing information overload. In this chapter, we will explore the benefits of mindfulness in the context of information consumption and discuss techniques that can be applied specifically to digital interactions.

Mindfulness has been proven to increase focus, reduce anxiety, and improve decision-making skills. In the digital age, where our attention is constantly pulled in multiple directions, cultivating mindfulness becomes even more crucial. We will explore techniques such as mindful scrolling, which involves being aware of our online behaviors and consciously choosing how we engage with digital content. By practicing mindful scrolling, we can avoid getting trapped in endless loops of mindless browsing and ensure that our online activities align with our intentions and values.

Additionally, we will discuss mindful social media usage, emphasizing the importance of being aware of our emotional responses to social media content and consciously choosing what we consume and share. By applying mindfulness to our social media interactions, we can avoid falling into the comparison trap, reduce feelings of inadequacy, and cultivate more positive and meaningful online experiences.

Furthermore, we will delve into mindful email management, highlighting the significance of being present and focused when dealing with our inboxes. Mindful email management involves setting specific times for checking and responding to emails, avoiding constant email notifications, and practicing active engagement with each message. By approaching email with mindfulness, we can reduce overwhelm, increase efficiency, and foster better communication.

## 3. Mindful Information Consumption:

In an era of information overload, cultivating a mindful approach to information consumption is essential for extracting meaningful insights and avoiding cognitive overload. In this chapter, we will discuss techniques for practicing mindful information consumption, enabling individuals to engage with knowledge more consciously and intentionally.

Selective reading is a fundamental aspect of mindful information consumption. Instead of trying to absorb every piece of information that comes our way, we should focus on selecting high-quality and relevant sources. By consciously choosing what we read, we can avoid being overwhelmed by an excess of information and ensure that our knowledge intake aligns with our interests and goals.

Critical evaluation of sources is another crucial skill for mindful information consumption. With the abundance of information available online, it is essential to be discerning and question the credibility and reliability of sources. We will explore strategies for evaluating sources, including fact-checking, considering the author's expertise and biases, and seeking multiple perspectives. By critically evaluating sources, we can avoid misinformation and develop a more accurate and nuanced understanding of the topics we explore.

Conscious engagement with content is also vital for mindful information consumption. This involves actively reflecting on and integrating the knowledge we encounter, rather than passively consuming it. We will discuss techniques such as summarizing key points, taking notes, and engaging in discussions or journaling to enhance our understanding and retention of information. By consciously engaging with content, we can transform information into knowledge and wisdom.

## 4. Cultivating Mindful Technology Use:

Mindful technology use involves intentionally engaging with technology consciously and purposefully. In this chapter, we will explore strategies for cultivating mindful technology habits, enabling individuals to develop a more balanced and intentional relationship with their devices.
One effective strategy is to turn off notifications that are not essential or relevant to our immediate needs. Constant notifications can be distracting and disrupt our focus, leading to a fragmented attention span. By selectively enabling notifications and minimizing their frequency, we can regain control over our attention and reduce the temptation to constantly check our devices.

Practicing single-tasking is another valuable habit for mindful technology use. Instead of trying to juggle multiple tasks simultaneously, we should focus on one task at a time, giving it our full attention. This approach promotes deep work, enhances productivity, and reduces the mental strain associated with multitasking. By dedicating our full attention to each task, we can also experience a greater sense of fulfillment and satisfaction.

Additionally, we can utilize productivity apps mindfully to enhance our efficiency and well-being. There are numerous apps available that can help manage tasks, improve focus, and promote mindfulness. However, it is essential to use these tools consciously and avoid becoming overly reliant on them. We will discuss strategies for incorporating productivity apps into our routines in a mindful and balanced way, ensuring that they support our well-being rather than adding to our digital dependencies.

**5. Integrating Digital and Offline Life:**

Finding a harmonious integration between our digital and offline lives is crucial for our overall well-being. In this chapter, we will discuss strategies for creating a healthy balance, enabling individuals to nurture a well-rounded life that includes both digital and offline experiences.

Scheduling regular offline activities is an essential aspect of integration. By consciously allocating time for activities such as exercise, hobbies, spending time with loved ones, or engaging in nature, we create opportunities for meaningful experiences and personal growth. These offline activities serve as a counterbalance to our digital engagements and help us reconnect with ourselves and the world around us.

Engaging in hobbies is another important element of integration. Hobbies provide a sense of fulfillment, joy, and personal expression. By pursuing activities that we are passionate about, whether it be painting, playing a musical instrument, gardening, or any other creative pursuit, we tap into our inner creativity and find respite from the constant demands of the digital world.Fostering meaningful face-to-face connections is also crucial for integration. While technology allows us to connect with others across the globe, it is important not to overlook the value of in-person interactions. We will explore strategies for nurturing deeper connections with friends, family, and communities, such as organizing regular social gatherings, participating in group activities, or volunteering. These offline connections provide a sense of belonging, support, and fulfillment that cannot be replicated solely through digital means. we have explored the concepts of digital detox and mindfulness as powerful tools for managing information overload and fostering a healthier relationship with technology. By implementing digital detox practices, setting boundaries with technology, cultivating mindfulness in the digital age, and integrating digital and offline experiences, we can regain control over our digital lives and cultivate a more balanced and mindful approach to knowledge consumption. In the following chapters, we will delve into the importance of nurturing intellectual curiosity and the development of healthy information consumption habits for lifelong learning in the age of knowledge overload.

# Chapter 6:

# Nurturing Intellectual Curiosity

Intellectual curiosity serves as a powerful driving force behind lifelong learning, personal growth, and the acquisition of knowledge. In this chapter, we will delve into the significance of nurturing and cultivating intellectual curiosity, especially in the face of information overload. By understanding the nature of intellectual curiosity, cultivating a curious mindset, embracing lifelong learning, exploring diverse topics, developing critical thinking skills, and cultivating joy in the learning process, we can foster intellectual curiosity and enhance our relationship with knowledge. Furthermore, we will also provide a glimpse into the subsequent chapters, which will delve into the development of healthy information consumption habits, ethical considerations in the digital age, and strategies for effective knowledge application in real-world contexts.

## 1. Understanding Intellectual Curiosity:

To begin our exploration, we will delve into the nature of intellectual curiosity and its role in human development. Intellectual curiosity is characterized by a strong desire to explore, inquire, and seek knowledge. We will investigate the benefits of intellectual curiosity, including enhanced creativity, critical thinking, and adaptability. By comprehending the importance of intellectual curiosity, we will be motivated to actively foster and nurture this trait within ourselves.

## 2. Cultivating a Curious Mindset:
Developing a curious mindset is essential for nurturing intellectual curiosity. We will delve into various strategies for cultivating curiosity, such as asking thought-provoking questions, embracing uncertainty, and maintaining an open mind. By doing so, we can ignite our creativity, drive innovation, and develop a lifelong love of learning fueled by curiosity.

## 3. Embracing Lifelong Learning:
Lifelong learning serves as both a mindset and a commitment to continuous growth and development.

We will explore the numerous benefits associated with embracing lifelong learning, including staying intellectually engaged, adapting to a rapidly changing world, and broadening our perspectives. Furthermore, we will provide practical approaches to lifelong learning, such as engaging in self-directed learning, seeking diverse learning opportunities, and harnessing the potential of new technologies for knowledge acquisition.

## 4. Exploring Diverse Topics:

Intellectual curiosity thrives when we venture beyond our comfort zones and explore diverse topics and disciplines. Recognizing the importance of interdisciplinary learning, we will discuss the benefits it offers. To broaden our intellectual horizons, we will explore strategies such as reading widely, attending lectures and workshops, engaging in conversations with experts, and taking advantage of online learning platforms. By doing so, we can enrich our understanding and foster intellectual curiosity.

## 5. Developing Critical Thinking Skills:

Critical thinking serves as a foundational skill for nurturing intellectual curiosity. We will delve into various techniques for developing critical thinking skills, such as analyzing information, evaluating evidence, and challenging assumptions. Through honing our critical thinking abilities, we can approach knowledge with a discerning eye, engage in deeper understanding, and navigate complex subjects effectively.

**6. Cultivating a Joyful Approach to Learning:**
Nurturing intellectual curiosity goes beyond merely acquiring knowledge; it involves finding joy in the learning process. We will emphasize the importance of intrinsic motivation, curiosity-driven projects, and embracing a growth mindset. By fostering a sense of joy and wonder in our pursuit of knowledge, we can sustain our intellectual curiosity and maintain a lifelong love of learning.

Throughout this chapter, we have explored the significance of nurturing intellectual curiosity amidst information overload. By cultivating a curious mindset, embracing lifelong learning, exploring diverse topics, developing critical thinking skills, and cultivating joy in the learning process, we can foster intellectual curiosity and enhance our relationship with knowledge. In the upcoming chapters, we will delve into the development of healthy information consumption habits, ethical considerations in the digital age, and strategies for effectively applying knowledge in real-world contexts. These topics will further empower us to navigate the challenges of the information

age while maximizing the benefits of intellectual curiosity and lifelong learning.

## Chapter 7:

## Building Healthy Information Consumption Habits

In the era of knowledge overload, it has become increasingly important to develop healthy information consumption habits. These habits are crucial for maintaining our mental well-being, nurturing our critical thinking skills, and enabling effective decision-making. In this chapter, we will delve into practical strategies that can aid in the development of habits promoting mindful, intentional, and responsible engagement with information. By adopting these strategies and building healthy information consumption habits, we can navigate the vast digital landscape with clarity, discernment, and a steadfast commitment to acquiring quality knowledge.

**1. Reflecting on Information Needs:**

Before immersing ourselves in the vast sea of available information, it is vital to reflect on our individual information needs and goals. Understanding the purpose behind our quest for information and setting specific objectives will be our first step. By engaging in this introspective process, we can clarify our information needs, narrow our focus, and shield ourselves from becoming overwhelmed by irrelevant or excessive information.

## 2. Setting Information Consumption Limits:

Just as it is crucial to set boundaries with technology, it is equally important to set limits on our information consumption. In this section, we will explore strategies to effectively manage the time we spend consuming information. Some of these strategies include allocating dedicated periods for information consumption, practicing intermittent fasting from information, and establishing information consumption quotas. By consciously setting limits, we can prevent information overload and cultivate a balanced approach to acquiring knowledge.

## 3. Diversifying Information Sources:

Relying solely on a single source or a limited set of sources can lead to biased and narrow perspectives. Recognizing this, we must emphasize the significance of diversifying our information sources to obtain a more comprehensive and balanced understanding. This section will explore various strategies for seeking out diverse perspectives, such as following reputable sources from different viewpoints, engaging with different media platforms, and actively seeking out underrepresented voices. By diversifying our sources, we can expand our knowledge horizons and gain a more nuanced perspective.

## 4. Practicing Skepticism and Fact-Checking:

In the face of rampant misinformation and disinformation, developing a skeptical mindset becomes crucial. This section will highlight the importance of fact-checking and verifying information before accepting it as true. We will delve into fact-checking techniques, reliable fact-checking organizations, and online tools that can assist us in discerning accurate information. By cultivating skepticism and incorporating fact-checking into our information consumption habits, we can shield ourselves from false or misleading information.

## 5. Engaging in Critical Evaluation:

Developing critical evaluation skills enables us to assess the credibility, bias, and relevance of the information we encounter. In this section, we will discuss strategies for critically evaluating sources, such as assessing the author's credentials, considering the source's reputation, and evaluating the supporting evidence. By actively engaging in critical evaluation, we can make informed judgments and discern high-quality information from the vast sea of available knowledge.

## 6. Practicing Digital Hygiene:

Digital hygiene involves maintaining a clean and healthy digital environment. This section will explore practices such as decluttering our digital devices, organizing digital files, and regularly reviewing and updating our digital subscriptions. By practicing digital hygiene, we can create a streamlined and manageable information ecosystem that supports effective information consumption. A clutter-free digital space can promote focus, reduce distractions, and enhance our overall digital well-being.

In this chapter, we have delved into practical strategies for building healthy information consumption habits in the digital age. By reflecting on our information needs, setting limits on consumption, diversifying our sources, practicing skepticism and fact-checking, engaging in critical evaluation, and practicing digital hygiene, we can cultivate mindful and responsible engagement with information. These habits will empower us to navigate the digital landscape, make informed decisions, and maintain a balanced approach to knowledge consumption. In the subsequent we will explore ethical considerations in the digital age and delve into strategies for effectively applying acquired knowledge in real-world contexts.

## Chapter 8:

## The Future of Knowledge and Information

As we delve into the rapidly advancing landscape of knowledge and information, it is crucial to delve deeper into the future implications and trends that will shape the way we acquire, process, and utilize knowledge. This chapter aims to provide an in-depth exploration of emerging technologies, evolving information ecosystems, and the ethical considerations that will shape the future of knowledge. By gaining a comprehensive understanding of these developments, we can equip ourselves to effectively navigate the future information landscape.

## 1. Artificial Intelligence and Knowledge Acquisition:

Artificial Intelligence (AI) has brought about a paradigm shift in the acquisition of knowledge. This section will delve into the multifaceted role of AI in automated knowledge extraction, machine learning, and natural language processing. We will explore the potential benefits and challenges associated with AI-driven knowledge acquisition and dissemination. Furthermore, we will examine the ethical considerations surrounding the use of AI, such as bias mitigation, transparency, and accountability.

## 2. Data Analytics and Knowledge Management:

Data analytics is revolutionizing the way we manage and extract insights from vast amounts of information. This section will explore the pivotal role of data analytics in knowledge management, encompassing areas such as data visualization, predictive analytics, and pattern recognition. Additionally, we will delve into the implications of data-driven decision-making and discuss the ethical considerations regarding data privacy, security, and responsible data usage.

## 3. Personalization and Customized Knowledge Delivery:

The future of knowledge dissemination is likely to embrace personalized and customized delivery systems. This section will focus on the emerging trends of recommendation algorithms, adaptive learning platforms, and personalized learning pathways. We will analyze the benefits associated with tailored knowledge delivery while addressing the challenges of ensuring inclusivity, and diverse perspectives, and mitigating the risks of information bubbles.

## 4. Open Access and Collaborative Knowledge Sharing:

Open access and collaborative knowledge sharing are redefining traditional knowledge ecosystems. This section will examine the rise of open educational resources, open-source platforms, and collaborative knowledge creation. We will delve into the potential benefits of democratized knowledge and discuss the challenges related to quality control, information credibility, and establishing trust in a decentralized knowledge landscape.

## 5. Ethical Considerations in Knowledge Creation and Consumption:

Ethical considerations play an increasingly vital role as we peer into the future. This section will explore pertinent issues such as information bias, algorithmic transparency, data privacy, and intellectual property rights. We will emphasize the significance of responsible knowledge creation and consumption and analyze the responsibilities of individuals, institutions, and policymakers in fostering an ethical information ecosystem.

## 6. Cultivating Digital Literacy and Critical Thinking:

In light of the evolving information landscape, digital literacy and critical thinking skills are of paramount importance. This section will underscore the significance of cultivating these skills to navigate complex information environments, combat misinformation, and make well-informed decisions. We will explore strategies for promoting digital literacy and critical thinking at the individual, educational, and societal levels, recognizing their pivotal role in empowering individuals to navigate the future information landscape effectively.

In this chapter, we have delved into the future of knowledge and information. By considering the impact of emerging technologies, evolving information ecosystems, and ethical considerations, we can better equip ourselves to tackle the challenges and embrace the opportunities that lie ahead. By cultivating digital literacy, and critical thinking, and adopting a mindful approach to knowledge consumption, we can confidently navigate the future with adaptability and a commitment to responsible and ethical engagement with knowledge. In the following chapters, we will delve into strategies for effectively applying knowledge in real-world contexts and underscore the importance of continuous learning in an era of perpetually evolving knowledge.

## Conclusion

This book has extensively explored the intricate phenomenon of knowledge overload and its profound impact on our lives. We have delved into a wide array of aspects related to this issue, ranging from the exponential growth of information to the psychology of information processing. We have discussed strategies for cultivating information literacy, managing information overload, and even engaging in a digital detox and mindfulness practices. Additionally, we have examined the importance of nurturing intellectual curiosity, fostering healthy information consumption habits, and contemplating the future of knowledge and information.

Through our exploration, it has become abundantly clear that knowledge overload is a multifaceted challenge that necessitates deliberate and mindful approaches to effectively navigate. The advent of the digital age has bestowed upon us an unparalleled wealth of knowledge, but it has also presented us with the critical task of filtering, evaluating, and processing information responsibly and ethically.

To flourish in the era of knowledge overload, we must cultivate information literacy skills. This involves the ability to access, evaluate, and efficiently apply information. Developing critical thinking skills is paramount to discerning reliable sources, recognizing biases, and critically analyzing the information presented to us. Moreover, we must remain cognizant of the detrimental consequences that can arise from information overload, including decreased productivity, heightened stress levels, and the rampant dissemination of misinformation. Throughout the pages of this book, we have explored numerous strategies and practices aimed at addressing knowledge overload. From embracing digital detoxification and practicing mindfulness to nurturing our innate intellectual curiosity and building healthy information consumption habits, we have provided readers with an array of tools and insights to help them navigate the vast digital landscape and make informed decisions.

Looking toward the future, we must consider the ever-evolving nature of knowledge and information. Emerging technologies, such as artificial intelligence and data analytics, will continue to shape how we acquire and process knowledge. As we progress, ethical considerations, open access, and collaborative knowledge sharing must remain at the forefront of our endeavors.

Ultimately, the journey to effectively manage knowledge overload is an ongoing process that extends throughout our lives. It requires a commitment to continuous learning, adaptability, and the pursuit of improvement. By staying informed, honing our critical thinking abilities, and fostering a mindful and responsible approach to information consumption, we can harness the boundless power of knowledge while skillfully avoiding its potential pitfalls.

In conclusion, knowledge overload should not be perceived as an insurmountable obstacle but rather as an impassioned call to action—an invitation to become active participants in our knowledge acquisition, processing, and utilization. By wholeheartedly embracing the principles and practices outlined in this book, we can empower ourselves to thrive in the era of knowledge overload and lead deeply fulfilling lives enriched by the immense resources available.